Seasons of Jam

WITH RECIPES CREATED BY

Jeannette Habit

PHOTOGRAPHED & EDITED BY

Karen Pavone

ADDITIONAL PHOTOGRAPHY BY

Jeannette Habit

DESIGNED & PUBLISHED BY

Gaye Allen

MEADOWLARK PUBLISHING

Contents

SPRING

Meyer Lemon Jam with Orange Blossom Honey 20
Strawberry & Vanilla Bean Preserve 22
Red Cherry Preserve with Kirsch Brandy 24
Strawberry-Rhubarb Jam 26

SUMMER

Wild Plum & Apple Jam with Vanilla Bean 30
Four Red Fruits Jam 32
Raspberry-White Peach Jam 34
Fig Jam with Vanilla Bean 36
Apricot-Nectarine Marmalade with Honey 38
Red Tomato & Apple Jam 40
Yellow & White Peach Jam 42
Summer Fruits Sangria 44

FALL

Apple-Cider Jelly 48
Pear, Apple & Candied Ginger Jam with Wild Honey 50
Pumpkin Butter with Dried Apricots & Citrus Zest 52
Spiced Pears in White Wine 54

WINTER

Spicy Red Pepper Jelly 58
Mango-Ginger Chutney 60
Clementine & Orange Marmalade 62
Pink Grapefruit Marmalade 64
Savory Cranberry-Apple-Orange Chutney 66

Above: Jeannette and her mother in Saigon in 1953

Left: Jeannette (seated center) with her mother (far left), two aunts and a cousin in Hanoi (circa 1943)

Right: Jeannette's father pictured outside the Continental Hotel in Saigon in 1954

Dedication

*This book is dedicated with love to my father,
Giang Nguyen (shown here in 1954),
with gratitude for making it possible from the start.
He worked as the Maitre d'Hotel
at the Continental Hotel in Saigon.*

Introduction

My love affair with preserves began, as many fateful moments do, in Paris.

I came to the City of Light to study the art of baking at one of its premier culinary schools–the Ecole Ritz-Escoffier–which is worlds away from the hectic urban streets of Hanoi, Vietnam where I was born. I wanted to follow in the footsteps of my beloved father, a talented Maître d'Hotel and chef, who ventured to Marseille in the 1930's to learn classic French cooking. His love of food inspired me then as it does to this day.

I enrolled in a six-week intensive pastry course, and whole-heartedly threw myself into the experience. One day, during a session on "fillings", our class tasted a lovely hand-crafted Mirabelle Plum jam made with crisp apples and a hint of vanilla. It was unlike anything I had ever sampled before; the perfect essence of rich, sun-ripened fruit captured in a jar.

That was it. I was smitten.

Upon completing the course I returned to the United States as a trained pastry chef and eventually opened my own dessert shop, La Royal Patisserie, in Tucson, Arizona. Yet despite its success, I remained obsessed with the memory of that incredible plum jam.

During my free time, I began experimenting in my home kitchen using preserve recipes I discovered while in France. I found that sourcing fruit seasonally not only made the best use of a plentiful harvest, but insured each jam was crafted with the freshest ingredients available. Soon after, I surrendered completely to the intoxicating aroma of the seasonal berries, stone fruit, and citrus that surrounded me as I worked. I was determined to recapture the taste I had experienced years earlier.

A decade and many test batches later, Jeannette's Jams has now grown into a "fruitful" business at local Marin County farmers' markets where I sell my unique seasonal preserves made in the age-old tradition of European grandmothers.

A Season of Jams brings you my best recipes, techniques, and tips for making your own delicious jams at home. With time and practice, I hope you will be inspired to create fresh, flavorful preserves like a pro!

Bon Appetite,

JEANNETTE N'GUYEN HABIT

The art of preserving fruit

Making delicious homemade preserves begins by observing this "Golden Rule": always start with the best quality, seasonal fruit available. Fruit is the primary ingredient and the main source of flavor in jam. Ideally, the fruit you choose should be Certified Organic, firm, perfectly ripe, fragrant, and at the peak of flavor. Using fruit that is bruised or past its prime will adversely affect the flavor, texture, and color of the end product.

Local farmers' markets are one of the best places to find fresh-picked fruits for jam making, and vendors often sell flats of ripe fruit for this purpose. The majority of the fruit and herbs used in my jams has been freshly harvested from local farms, orchards, and gardens. Following this field-to-jar approach whenever possible will help you achieve superior tasting results.

Jeannette says

"I highly recommend reading the recipe to thoroughly familiarize yourself with the process before you begin cooking. Next, prep and pre-measure all the ingredients. Lastly, gather all the necessary equipment/tools using the guide on page 13. Following this routine will help you stay organized and avoid surprises."

CORRECT CONSISTENCY

MORE COOKING NEEDED

The "Set Point"

It is important to constantly monitor the temperature of the jam as it cooks. Overcooking may result in gummy texture and off-color, while undercooking will produce a runny consistency. For best results, insert a candy thermometer into the jam to determine when the mixture has reached the proper set point of 210°F (105°C).

To test if the jam is done, put a quarter spoonful of the mixture on a chilled saucer. Place the saucer in the freezer for five minutes. If the jam holds its shape and doesn't readily drip when the saucer is tilted, it is ready to jar!

About Pectin

All fruits naturally contain pectin; a gelling agent that helps to thicken and solidify the fruit juices in jam as it cooks. Different fruits have higher or lower pectin content which must be balanced with sugar and acidity to achieve the desired consistency in the finished preserve.

The list in the panel opposite can be used as a basic guide:

Though commercial pectin powders and liquids are widely available in many grocery stores, most are produced in Europe and imported to the United States. These products have a limited shelf life and will lose their ability to gel over time. I've found making fresh homemade pectin from under-ripe Granny Smith apples yields a better result.

HIGH ACID FRUITS

LEMONS • BLACK CURRANT
GOOSEBERRY • KUMQUATS
ORANGES • GRAPEFRUITS
PLUMS • GREEN TOMATOES

LOW ACID FRUITS

NECTARINE • PEACH
QUINCE • STRAWBERRY
KIWI • MANGO • MELONS
PEARS • FIGS

HIGH PECTIN FRUITS

BLACK CURRANT
HUCKLEBERRY • LEMONS
GUAVA • GOOSEBERRY
ORANGES • QUINCE
GRAPEFRUIT • PLUMS
GREEN APPLE

LOW PECTIN FRUITS

PINEAPPLE • NECTARINES
CHERRIES • MELONS
PEARS • RHUBARB
FIGS • STRAWBERRY
RED & GREEN TOMATOES

Perfect Pectin

This "pectin stock" can be added to recipes that call for low-pectin fruits, and will keep up to six months in the refrigerator.

2 ½ lbs. under-ripe Granny Smith apples (preferably organic)
1 cup raw cane sugar
6 cups water
Juice 1 lemon
Cheesecloth

YIELDS 4 X 9 OZ JARS

1 Rinse the apples in cold water. Remove the stems and cut into quarters leaving the peels intact.

2 Place the apples in a large pot and completely cover the fruit with 6 cups of water.

3 Bring to a boil, then reduce to low heat and simmer for 40 minutes until the apples are soft.

4 Place a fine-mesh chinois sieve in a large bowl. Pour the cooked apples into the sieve and press lightly with a wooden spoon to release the juice. Use cheesecloth to filter the juice a second time until it runs clear. You should have about 4 cups of juice.

5 Pour the apple juice into a wide preserve pan. Add the sugar and lemon juice.

6 Bring the mixture to a boil, stirring gently and skimming off any foam that collects on the surface.

7 Reduce the heat to medium and continue cooking for 25 minutes. Skim foam if necessary. Simmer until the juice is thickened and reduced to 2 ½ cups of pectin.

8 Use a candy thermometer to check the set point (210°F). Remove from heat.

9 Slowly ladle the pectin into warm sterilized jars. Wipe the jar rims clean with a moist paper towel and screw the lids on firmly.

10 Let the pectin cool completely at room temperature. Refrigerate and use within six months.

A Note On Sugar

Sugar is a natural preservative that works with pectin to enhance the flavor and texture of preserves. I always use raw organic cane sugar because it dissolves quickly and reduces the formation of bubbles in the jam. Honey is another natural sweetener that may be used if preferred. No matter which type of sweetener you choose, be sure it is of the highest quality.

As a rule of thumb, I use thirty-five percent sugar per batch of jam (one batch is approximately 7-9 pounds of fruit). Adding minimal sugar is not only healthier, but allows the natural sweetness of the fruit to completely shine through.

By contrast, most of the jams produced in France are about 60% sugar. To adjust for using less sweetener, I reduce my jam slowly over low heat to intensify the natural fruit flavors. I repeat this process several times for each batch. As the jam slowly cooks down, the fruit gradually absorbs the sugar but keeps its texture. I also add lemon juice to prevent oxidation and enhance the color of the finished preserves.

When cooked slowly in small batches, the fruit transforms into the delectable jams, jellies, marmalades, and chutneys outlined in this book. To understand the qualities of each type of preserve, I have included these descriptions.

JAM
Jam is made of crushed, diced, or chopped fruits that are cooked with sugar to create a firm textured, easy-to-spread preserve.

JELLY
Jelly is a sweet, translucent preserve made from fruit juice and sugar. A good jelly is clear, sparkling, and has a clean, fruity flavor.

MARMALADE
Marmalade is made from fruit mixed with juice and citrus peel that has been boiled in sugar and water. The citrus peel imparts a distinctive bitter taste that is a trademark of this style of preserve. It can be made from all varieties of citrus including lemons, limes, rose grapefruit, Clémentine, and sweet orange varieties like Mineola and/or Cara Cara.

CHUTNEY
Chutney is a chunky relish made of fruit, spices, herbs, sugar, sea salt and wine or apple cider vinegar. Mango fruit is a popular choice for making chutney, but this preserve can also be made with a variety of dried fruits.

Equipment

Investing in a few basic pieces of good equipment will bring you a lifetime of enjoyment in the kitchen. Quality cookware may cost a bit more, but it will last longer and makes the tasks at hand much easier.

I prefer the superior heat distribution of wide, shallow copper preserve pans for cooking jam. Copper is also well-suited to both gas and electric cooktops. Stainless steel stockpots are acceptable, but the fruit will stick to the bottom during cooking.

Note: Do not use copper pans for macerating. The natural acids released by the fruit may oxidize and cause pits in the pan.

A stainless steel skimmer is my favorite all-purpose tool for stirring and checking the consistency of jam as it cooks. The skimmer also makes easy work of removing bits of whole spice and herbs added in some recipes.

Use this comprehensive checklist of tools as a guide for making jam.

Jeannette says

"It is best to lay out all the needed equipment before you begin cooking so you have everything close at hand."

- Cutting board
- Sharp paring knives
- Standing colander
- Food mill
- Large mixing bowls
- Kitchen scale
- Fine-mesh chinois sieve
- Cheesecloth
- Citrus zester
- Vegetable peeler
- Wooden spoons
- Copper preserve pan
- Stainless steel skimmer
- Tongs or a jar lifter
- Parchment paper
- Kitchen towels
- Candy thermometer
- Jam funnel
- Stainless steel ladle
- Glass jars (various sizes)
- Button safety lids
- Labels

Using a Food Mill

A food mill is the kitchen workhorse for making preserves. This indispensable tool, which is part grinder and part strainer, easily and efficiently removes fruit seeds, pulp, and skins to create a smooth finished puree.

Food mills are generally made of stainless steel or aluminum and have three parts: a bowl to collect the finished juice and sauce; interchangeable perforated disks with different sized holes; and a turn crank fitted with a metal blade that crushes the fruit and forces it through the chosen disk.

I regularly use a food mill to process tomatoes and berries for the recipes in this book. This time-saving device makes short work of transforming fruit into sauce, paste, and puree that would take far longer if done by hand.

Sterilizing jars

Glass preserve jars and lids must be properly sterilized to insure the finished jam can be successfully stored.

1 First, visually inspect each jar for cracks or chips on the rim and discard any that are flawed.

2 Next, wash the jars and lids by hand in hot soapy water and rinse them thoroughly with hot water.

3 Place the washed jars upright in a single layer in a large stockpot. Fill the pot with water until the jars are completely submerged. Bring to a boil over high heat. Boil the jars for 10 minutes to sterilize.

4 Turn off the heat, but keep the jars submerged in the hot water until you are ready to fill them.

5 Place the washed lids in a sauce pan and cover them with water. Bring to a simmer over medium heat for 5 minutes.

6 Turn off the heat, but keep the lids submerged in hot water until you are ready to cap the jars.

Note: It is acceptable to recycle canning jars and rings for future use, but canning lids are made to seal only once and may not be reused. Put a new lid on each jar you process.

Filling the jars

1 Use tongs or a jar lifter to carefully remove the glass jars from the hot water bath, and empty them of all water.

2 Place the jars mouth-side-up on a clean kitchen towel. Insert a jam funnel into the mouth of each jar and fill to ¼" from the top with hot jam.

3 Run a table knife around the inside of the jar to encourage any remaining bubbles to escape.

4 Wipe off excess drips around the rim of the jar with a moist paper towel.

5 Use tongs to retrieve a lid from the warm water and place it on top of the jar. Secure in place with the screw rim provided and tighten snugly.

6 Finally, turn the jars upside down for about 30 minutes to encourage any remaining air bubbles trapped in the jam to escape (a tip I learned in cooking school). As the jam cools, the natural pectin will develop to a perfect consistency. Continue to rest at room temperature for 24 hours.

7 Store the preserves in a cool dark place and consume within the specified time period.

meyer lemon jam with orange blossom honey

The sweet flavor and mild acidity of Meyer lemons blends perfectly with honey in this fragrant citrus jam.

Ingredients

3 lbs. Meyer lemons
1 lb. Granny Smith apples
2 cups raw cane sugar
Juice 2 lemons
½ cup orange blossom honey
½ cup water

YIELDS 6 X 6 OZ JARS

Jeannette says

"this Meyer lemon jam makes a delicious base for lemon tarts!"

day one

1 Rinse the apples in cold water. Remove the stems and cut them in quarters without peeling.

2 Put the apples in a large pot and cover them with water. Bring to a rolling boil, then reduce to medium heat and simmer for 30 minutes until the apples are soft.

3 Set a fine-mesh chinois sieve in a large pan and pour the apple mixture into the sieve. Lightly press fruit with the back of a wooden spoon to release the pectin stock into the collection pan.

4 Squeeze the juice from 2 lemons. Measure 1 cup lemon juice and set aside. Place the lemon seeds in a cheesecloth bag and set aside.

5 Wash the Meyer lemons in cold water and slice into very thin rounds.

6 In a preserve pan, simmer the sliced lemons with 1 cup sugar and ½ cup water for 25 minutes until the rounds are translucent.

7 Add the lemon juice, cheesecloth bag with lemon seeds, apple pectin stock, and 2 tablespoons orange blossom honey. Bring to a simmer on low heat, stirring gently with a wooden spoon and skimming off foam. Continue cooking for 25 minutes.

8 Pour the mixture into a bowl. Cover with parchment paper and refrigerate overnight.

day two

9 Pour the preparation into a preserve pan. Bring to a boil and cook on high heat for 10 minutes, stirring frequently and skimming as necessary.

10 Add the remaining orange blossom honey and reduce heat to low. Continue cooking for 15 minutes more. The jam will become thick and syrupy with a clear, blushing orange color.

11 Remove the cheesecloth bag. Check the set point with a candy thermometer (210°F).

12 Slowly ladle the jam into warm sterilized jars. Wipe the jar rims clean with a moist paper towel and screw the lids on tight. Store in a cool dark place and consume within six months.

strawberry & vanilla bean preserve

The word "macerate" means to soak in fluid. This process softens the fruit as it slowly absorbs the flavor of the liquid.

Ingredients

4 lbs. ripe strawberries
2 cups raw cane sugar
Juice 1 lemon
1 vanilla bean
½ cup white grape juice or water

YIELDS 6 X 6 OZ JARS

Jeannette says

"smaller sized strawberries may be used whole in this recipe, while larger berries should be quartered."

day one

1. Rinse whole strawberries in cold water and dry them carefully. Remove the stems and cut into quarters.

2. In a large bowl combine the strawberries, sugar, lemon juice, vanilla bean and grape juice or water. Cover the mixture with a sheet of parchment paper and macerate for 8 hours.

day two

3. Pour the macerated fruit into a preserve pan and bring to a boil. Cook on medium heat for 15 minutes, stirring gently and skimming off any foam that collects on the surface.

4. Pour this preparation into a bowl and cool to room temperature. Cover with parchment paper and refrigerate overnight.

day three

5. Place a chinois sieve over a large preserve pan and pour the fruit mixture into the sieve to collect the juice. Set aside the fruit solids.

6. Bring the berry juice to a boil and continue cooking over high heat, skimming excess foam as necessary. Monitor the temperature with a candy thermometer until it reaches the set point (210°F).

7. Add the reserved fruit solids to the syrup and return to a boil. Skim as needed and stir gently for 5 minutes. The jam should be glossy and translucent.

8. Remove jam from heat and ladle into warm sterilized jars. Wipe the jar rims clean with a moist paper towel and screw the lids on tight. Turn the jars upside down for 30 minutes. Store in a cool dark place and consume within six months.

red cherry preserve with kirsch brandy

Brandy adds dimension to this intensely flavorful jam starring summer's first stone fruit.

Ingredients

3 lbs. red cherries
2 cups raw cane sugar
Juice 1 lemon
¼ cup "Kirsch" brandy

YIELDS 6 X 6 OZ JARS

Jeannette says

"kirsch is a cherry liqueur made from cherries that enhances the fruit flavors in this gorgeous, deep-red preserve."

day one

1. Rinse the cherries in cold water and dry them in a towel. Remove the stems, pits, and cut them in half.

2. Combine the cherries, lemon juice, and sugar in a bowl. Macerate at room temperature for 30 minutes.

3. Pour the preparation into a preserve pan. Bring to a simmer on medium heat and cook for 30 minutes, stirring gently and skimming off any foam that collects on the surface.

4. Pour the mixture into a bowl. Cover with parchment paper and refrigerate overnight.

day two

5. Pour the fruit mixture into a preserve pan and bring to a boil on high heat for 5-10 minutes, stirring gently and skimming foam as necessary.

6. Reduce heat to simmer and continue cooking for 20 minutes, stirring frequently. The jam will darken and become syrupy.

7. Add Kirsch and cook for another 10 minutes, skimming off foam. Check the set point with a candy thermometer (210°F).

8. Slowly ladle the jam into warm sterilized jars. Wipe the jar rims clean with a moist paper towel and screw the lids on tight. Turn the jars upside down for 30 minutes. Store in a cool dark place and consume within six months.

strawberry-rhubarb jam

This quintessential combination of sweet fresh strawberries and tart rhubarb is everyone's favorite!

Ingredients

3 lbs. strawberries
1 lb. rhubarb
2 cups raw cane sugar
Juice 1 lemon

YIELDS 6 X 6 OZ JARS

Jeannette says

"for this recipe, I prefer to use the thin, slender green stalks of rhubarb which are less watery and slightly acidic."

day one

1. Rinse rhubarb in cold water and halve the stalks lengthwise. Do not peel. Cut into small dice.

2. Gently rinse strawberries in cold water. Dry and cut them in half.

3. In a large bowl, combine the strawberries and rhubarb with the sugar and lemon juice. Cover with parchment paper and macerate for 20 minutes.

4. Pour the mixture into a preserve pan and bring to a simmer for 15 minutes.

5. Pour into a large bowl and cover with parchment paper. Allow the mixture to rest overnight in the refrigerator.

day two

6. Pour the preparation into a preserve pan and bring to a boil. Stir gently using a wooden spoon and skim off any foam that collects on the surface. Continue cooking on high heat for 5-10 minutes, stirring constantly.

7. Turn the heat to low and carefully check the jam. It should be slightly jelled. Check the set point with a candy thermometer (210°F).

8. Ladle the jam into warm, sterilized jars. Wipe the jar rims clean with a moist paper towel and screw the lids on tight. Turn the jars upside down for 30 minutes. Store in a cool dark place and consume within six months.

wild plum & apple jam with vanilla bean

Savor summer's plum harvest at its peak of flavor with this delicious recipe.

Ingredients

3 lbs. red or black plums

1 lb. Golden Delicious apples

2 cups raw cane sugar

Juice 1 lemon

2 vanilla beans

YIELDS 6 X 6 OZ JARS

Jeannette says

"reserve the pieces of vanilla bean pod and add them to each jar of jam as a lovely decorative touch."

day one

1. Rinse the plums in cold water. Peel, remove the pits, and cut into thin slices.

2. Wash the apples. Peel, core, and chop into pieces.

3. In a bowl, combine the sliced plums, chopped apples, lemon juice, and sugar. Split the vanilla bean pod lengthwise and scrape the seeds into the fruit. Add the pod to the fruit mixture, and macerate at room temperature for 30 minutes.

4. Pour the preparation into a preserve pan and bring to a simmer, stirring gently with a wooden spoon. Skim off any foam that collects on the surface. Continue cooking for 30 minutes.

5. Pour the mixture into a bowl and cover with parchment paper. Refrigerate overnight.

day two

6. Pour the fruits mixture into a preserve pan and bring to a boil on high heat for 5-10 minutes, stirring gently and skimming off any foam.

7. Reduce heat to medium-low and simmer until the jam thickens and becomes glossy. Remove the vanilla bean and set aside. Continue cooking on low heat for another 10 minutes.

8. Check the set point with a candy thermometer (210°F). Slowly ladle the jam into warm sterilized jars. Wipe the jar rims clean with a moist paper towel and screw the lids on tight. Turn the jars upside down for 30 minutes. Store in cool dark place and consume within six months.

four red fruits jam

The perfect marriage of strawberries, raspberries, cherries, and blueberries comes together in this exceptionally flavorful preserve

Ingredients

2 lbs. strawberries
2 lbs. raspberries
½ lb. cherries
½ lb. blueberries
Juice 1 Meyer lemon
3 cups raw cane sugar
1 vanilla bean

YIELDS 6 X 6 OZ JARS

Jeannette says

"use a food mill fitted with a fine disk to make quick work of removing the raspberry seeds with ease."

day one

1 Rinse the strawberries in cold water. Dry and cut them in half.

2 Rinse the cherries in cold water. Dry, stem, and pit them.

3 Quickly rinse the blueberries. Set aside.

4 To preserve the fragrance and flavor of the raspberries, do not rinse them. Place a food mill fitted with a fine disk over a large pan. Pour the whole raspberries into the mill and slowly turn to separate the seeds from the juice. Discard the seeds.

5 Combine all the fruits with sugar and lemon juice in a large bowl. Cover with parchment and macerate for 1 hour.

6 Pour macerated fruits into a preserve pan and bring to a simmer for 20 minutes, stirring gently with a wooden spoon and skimming off any foam that collects on the surface. Pour mixture into a bowl and cover with parchment paper. Refrigerate overnight.

day two

7 Place a fine mesh chinois sieve in a preserve pan and pour the fruit mixture into the sieve, pressing lightly with a wooden spoon to release the juice. Reserve the fruit solids and vanilla bean. Set aside.

8 Pour the juice into a large pot and bring to a boil for 10 minutes. The liquid will be thick and syrupy.

9 Add the reserved fruit solids and vanilla bean. Return to a boil. Continue cooking on high heat for 5-10 minutes, stirring constantly. Skim foam as needed. The mixture should have a loose, jam-like consistency. Check the set point with a candy thermometer (210°F).

10 Turn the heat to low. Remove the vanilla bean and cut the pod into small pieces to decorate each jar. Ladle the jam into warm, sterilized jars. Wipe the jar rims with a moist paper towel and screw the lids on tight. Turn the jars upside down for 30 minutes. Store in a cool dark place and consume within six months.

raspberry-white peach jam

This combination of sweet, white-fleshed peaches and tart raspberries makes a heavenly topping on vanilla ice cream!

Ingredients

3½ lbs. ripe, firm white peaches

3 lbs. raspberries

2 cups raw cane sugar

Grated zest ½ lemon and ½ orange

Juice 1 lemon

YIELDS 6 X 6 OZ JARS

Jeannette says

"avoid rinsing the raspberries to preserve their delicate flavor and fragrance."

day one

1. Bring a large pot of water to a rolling boil. Wash the peaches in cold water and drop them, one by one, into the boiling water. Blanch just until the skins are softened (approximately 1-2 minutes). Using a slotted spoon, removed the peaches and plunge them into a cold water bath.

2. Peel the peaches, remove and discard pits, and cut them into dice with a sharp knife.

3. Pour whole, unwashed raspberries into the bowl of a food mill fitted with a fine disk and process to remove the seeds. Pour the puree into a bowl and set aside.

4. Use a zester to grate the peels of ½ lemon and ½ orange. Set aside.

5. Combine the peaches, raspberry puree, lemon juice, citrus zest, and sugar in a large preserve pan. Bring to a simmer on medium-heat and cook for about 25 minutes, stirring gently with a wooden spoon and skimming off any foam that collects on the surface.

6. Pour the fruit mixture into a bowl. Cover with parchment paper and refrigerate overnight.

day two

7. In a preserve pan, bring the mixture to a boil on high heat for 10 minutes, stirring constantly and skimming off any foam.

8. Reduce heat to medium-low and continue cooking until the jam thickens. Reduce heat to low and cook for another 10 minutes. Check the set point with a candy thermometer (210°F).

9. Slowly ladle the jam into warm sterilized jars. Wipe the jar rims clean with a moist paper towel and screw the lids on tight. Turn the jars upside down for 30 minutes. Store in a cool dark place and consume within six months.

fig jam with vanilla bean

Serve this rich, delicious jam as a condiment with English shortbread cookies for tea or dessert.

Ingredients

3 lbs. fresh figs

2 cups raw cane sugar

Juice 1 lemon

2 tablespoons pure vanilla extract

1 vanilla bean* (optional)

YIELDS 6 X 6 OZ JARS

Jeannette says

"select small, purple-skinned figs with red flesh. They make the richest flavored jam with a beautiful finished color!"

day one

1. Rinse the figs in cold water and dry them in a towel. Remove the stems and slice them.

2. In a bowl combine fig slices, sugar, lemon juice, and vanilla*.
*Note: If using vanilla bean, split the pod lengthwise and scrape the seeds into the mixture. Add the pod to the fruit mixture.

3. Cover with parchment paper and macerate for one hour.

4. Pour the fruit preparation into a preserve pan and bring to a simmer, stirring gently. Skim as needed and continue cooking for 25 minutes.

5. Pour the mixture back into a bowl. Cover with parchment paper and Refrigerate over night.

day two

6. Pour the mixture into a preserve pan and bring to a boil, skimming as needed. Cook on high heat for 10-15 minutes, stirring constantly.

7. If using vanilla bean, remove the pod altogether or cut into ½ inch pieces and add to the jars as decoration. Reduce the heat to low and continue to cook down the jam until the liquid is thick and syrupy. Check the set point with a candy thermometer (210°F).

8. Ladle the jam into warm, sterilized jars. Wipe the jar rims clean with a moist paper towel and screw the lids on tight. Turn the jars upside down for 30 minutes. Store in a cool dark place and consume within six months.

apricot-nectarine marmalade with honey

These lovely summer stone fruits blend together perfectly in this silky marmalade.

Ingredients

3 lbs. apricots
1½ lbs. nectarines
1 cup raw cane sugar
½ cup honey
Juice 1 lemon

YIELDS 6 X 6 OZ JARS

Jeannette says

"try this as a topping on butter-pecan ice cream for dessert. It's delicious!"

day one

1. Rinse apricots in cold water. Remove the pits and cut them into dice.

2. Bring a large pot of water to a rolling boil. Add the nectarines, one by one, and blanch approximately 1 minute until the skins are just softened. Use a slotted spoon to remove the nectarines and plunge them into a cold water bath.

3. Remove the outer skins and pits. Cut the fruit into sections. Combine apricots and nectarines with the sugar and macerate for 30 minutes.

4. In a large preserve pan, combine the fruit mixture with honey and lemon juice. Bring to a simmer, stirring gently and skimming off any foam that collects on the surface. Cook for about 30 minutes until the sugar dissolves.

5. Pour the mixture into a bowl and cover with parchment paper. Refrigerate overnight.

day two

6. Pour the preparation into a preserve pan and bring to a boil, stirring frequently. Skim off foam and continue cooking on high heat for 5-10 minutes, stirring gently.

7. Reduce the heat to simmer. The marmalade will become thick and syrupy. Check the set point with a candy thermometer (210°F).

8. Slowly ladle the marmalade into warm sterilized jars. Wipe the jar rims clean with a moist paper towel and screw the lids on tight. Turn the jars upside down for 30 minutes. Store in a cool dark place and consume within six months.

red tomato & apple jam

Ripe red summer tomatoes make a savory-sweet jam that elevates simple ingredients to heavenly heights.

Ingredients

3½ lbs. tomatoes (preferably Beefsteak variety)

1 lb. apples (about 3 medium Golden Delicious)

Juice 1 lemon

2 cups raw cane sugar

1 vanilla bean

YIELDS 6 X 6 OZ JARS

Jeannette says

"for a decorative touch, add pieces of vanilla bean to each jar of jam."

day one

1. Bring a large pot of water to a rolling boil. Drop the tomatoes in, one by one, and blanch just until the skins are softened (about 1-2 minutes).

2. Use a slotted spoon to remove the tomatoes and plunge them into a cold water bath. Remove the skins and seeds. Cut into quarters and squeeze out excess juice. Place tomatoes in a colander to drain.

3. Cut the drained tomatoes into dice.

4. Rinse apples in cold water. Peel and remove the stems, core, and seeds. Cut into thin slices.

5. Combine the tomatoes, sliced apples, sugar, and lemon juice in a large preserve pan. Split vanilla bean lengthwise and scrape the seeds into the mixture. Add the pod. Bring to a simmer, stirring gently and skimming off any foam that collects on the surface. Simmer for about 25 minutes.

6. Pour mixture into a bowl and cover with parchment paper. Refrigerate overnight.

day two

7. Set a chinois sieve in a large pan and pour the preparation into the sieve, pressing on the fruit with the back of a wooden spoon to extract the juice. Reserve the solids.

8. Bring the juice to a boil. Skim foam as necessary, and continue cooking until the juice is reduced to 1 cup of syrup.

9. Pour the reserved fruit solids into the syrup and reduce the heat to medium-low. Continue cooking for another 20 minutes, stirring gently and skimming foam as necessary. The jam will become thick, smooth, and syrupy.

10. Reduce to low-heat. Remove the vanilla bean pod and cut into 1" segments. Set aside. Check the set point with a candy thermometer (210°F).

11. Slowly ladle hot jam into warm sterilized jars. Add vanilla bean segments for a decorative touch if desired. Wipe the jar rims clean with a moist paper towel and screw the lids on tight. Turn the jars upside down for 30 minutes. Store in cool dark place and consume within six months.

yellow and white peach jam

This jam pairs well with artisan cheese for a beautiful appetizer that's sure to delight. It's the essence of summer in a jar!

Ingredients

2 lbs. yellow peaches
2 lbs. white peaches
2 cups raw cane sugar
Juice 1 lemon

YIELDS 6 X 6 OZ JARS

Jeannette says

"the sweet, delicate flavor of white peaches mixed with the tangy acidity of yellow peaches make a beautifully balanced jam."

day one

1. Rinse the peaches in cold water. Bring a large pot of water to a rolling boil. Drop the peaches, one by one, into the boiling water for 1-2 minutes just until the skins are softened.

2. Use a slotted spoon to remove the peaches and plunge them into a cold water bath. Remove the skins and pits. Cut into large dice.

3. In a preserve pan, combine the fruits with the sugar and lemon juice. Bring to a simmer, stirring gently with a wooden spoon and skimming off any foam that collects on the surface. Continue cooking for 30 minutes on medium heat.

4. Pour the fruit mixture into a bowl. Cover with parchment paper and refrigerate overnight.

day two

5. Pour the fruit mixture into a preserve pan. Bring to a boil on high heat for 5-10 minutes, stirring gently and skimming off any foam on the surface.

6. Reduce heat to a simmer and continue cooking until jam darkens and the syrup becomes thick and glossy. Check the set point with a candy thermometer (210°F).

7. Simmer for another 5 minutes. Slowly ladle the jam into warm sterilized jars. Wipe the jar rims clean with a moist paper towel and screw the lids on tight. Turn the jars upside down for 30 minutes. Store in cool dark place and consume within six months.

summer fruits sangria

This refreshing, fruity sip is the perfect luncheon or after-dinner drink on hot summer days.

Ingredients

2 lbs. mixed fresh stone fruits (cherries, plums, peaches, apricots and/or grapes)

1 quart Classic Simple Syrup (recipe opposite)

4 cups raw cane sugar

1 quart water

1 quart premium vodka

YIELDS 3½ QUARTS

Jeannette says

"for a heavenly dessert, ladle a few of the fruits into a small bowl of ice cream, sorbet or cake and top with a little bit of the sangria."

day one

To make Classic Simple Syrup:

1. Combine the sugar and water in a large saucepan. Bring to a boil over high heat, stirring with a wooden spoon until all the sugar is dissolved.

2. Set aside to cool. Store sealed simple syrup in the refrigerator for up to two weeks.

day two

3. Layer unpeeled fruits in a large, widemouthed glass beverage container. Cherries and grapes should remain whole; halve or quarter other fruits.

4. Pour equal portions of cooled simple syrup and vodka over the fruits. Cover securely with plastic wrap and weight with a small bowl or plate to completely immerse the fruits in liquid.

5. Set aside in a cool, dry place for at least 2 months to develop. As the sangria ripens, the liquid will take on a rose-colored hue.

apple-cider jelly

This lightly spiced jelly makes a perfect glaze for fruit tarts.

Ingredients

4 ½ lbs. Granny Smith apples

4 cups apple cider

2 cups water

3 cups raw cane sugar

Juice 1 lemon

YIELDS 6 X 6 OZ JARS

Jeannette says

"this jelly is delicious paired with notes of fresh mint, basil, or jalapeño pepper."

day one

1. Rinse the apples in cold water. Do not peel. Remove the stems, and cut into quarters.

2. Place the apples in a preserve pan and cover them with the apple cider and water. Bring to a boil and reduce the heat to medium-low. Simmer for 1 hour until soft.

3. Place a fine-mesh chinois sieve in a large pan and pour the mixture into the sieve. Press the fruit lightly with a wooden spoon to release the juice.

4. Filter the juice through cheesecloth a second time until it is free of debris. Place in refrigerator to rest overnight.

day two

5. Measure 5 cups of the strained juice into a preserve pan. Add the lemon juice and 2 ½ cups sugar. Bring to a boil for 10 minutes, stirring constantly and skimming off any foam that collects on the surface.

6. Reduce to medium heat and continue cooking. Add the remaining ½ cup of sugar. Bring to a rolling boil for another 10 minutes, stirring constantly.

7. To test the jelly, take a half spoonful of the mixture and let it cool to room temperature on the spoon. If it thickens and jells, it is ready to jar.

8. Use a jam funnel and ladle to fill the warm sterilized jars with jelly. Wipe the jar rims clean with a moist paper towel and screw the lids on tight. Turn the jars upside down for 30 minutes. Store in a cool dark place and consume within six months.

pear, apple & candied ginger jam with wild honey

The sweet heat of crystalized ginger and pungent fresh ginger in this recipe dances on the tongue.

Ingredients

3½ lbs. Bartlett pears (6 medium pears)

1 lb. apples (preferably Golden Delicious)

1¾ cups raw cane sugar

½ cup wildflower honey

¼ cup crystallized candied ginger, finely chopped

¼ cup fresh ginger, finely chopped

Juice 1 lemon

½ cup homemade fruit pectin stock (optional)

YIELDS 6 X 6 OZ JARS

day one

1. Wash the pears and apples in cold water. Remove the peel, stem, and core of the fruit and cut into thin slices.

2. Combine the pear and apple slices, lemon juice, honey, and candied & fresh ginger in a preserve pan. Allow the mixture to macerate for 30 minutes.

3. Bring the preparation to a simmer on medium heat and cook for about 25 minutes, stirring gently with a wooden spoon and skimming off any foam that collects on the surface.

4. Pour the mixture into a bowl and cover with parchment paper. Refrigerate overnight.

day two

5. Bring the mixture to a boil on high heat for 10 minutes. Add ½ cup fruit pectin stock if needed, stir gently, and skim off any foam.

6. Reduce heat to medium-low and continue cooking for about 20 minutes until a candy thermometer inserted in the mixture registers the set point of 210°F.

7. Slowly ladle the jam into warm, sterilized jars. Wipe the jar rims clean with a moist paper towel and screw the lids on tight. Turn the jars upside down for 30 minutes. Store in a cool dark place and consume within six months.

Jeannette says

"this savory and slightly spicy jam perfectly complements poultry."

pumpkin butter with dried apricots & citrus zests

Capture the flavors of fall with this exquisite pumpkin butter.

Ingredients

4 lbs. pumpkin (or Red Kuri squash)

1 cup dried apricots; julienne cut

Juice 1 orange

Juice 1 lemon

grated zest ½ lemon and ½ orange

2 ½ cups raw cane sugar

1 cup homemade pectin stock (page 11)

YIELDS 6 X 6 OZ JARS

Jeannette says

"I always use Red Kuri squash in this recipe for its sweet flavor and soft texture."

day one

1 Preheat oven to 350°F.

2 Soak the dried apricot slices in warm water for 15 minutes. Drain in a colander.

3 Split the pumpkins in half and cut each into 4 wedges. Scrape out the seeds and pulp. Place wedges on a baking sheet and cover with foil. Bake for 20 minutes on the center oven rack until soft. Cool to room temperature.

4 Remove the outer peel of each wedge using a serrated knife and discard peel. Puree the pumpkin in a food processor until smooth.

5 Combine the pureed pumpkin, apricots, lemon juice, orange juice, 1 cup sugar, and citrus zest in a preserve pan and bring to a simmer. Stir gently with a wooden spoon to mix and skim off foam as necessary. Continue cooking for 30 minutes.

6 Remove mixture from the stove and pour in a bowl. Cover with parchment paper and refrigerate overnight.

day two

7 Pour the preparation into a preserve pan. Add the pectin stock and 1 ½ cups sugar. Bring to a simmer on medium-low heat and cook for 30 minutes, stirring gently with a wooden spoon and skimming off foam as necessary. The mixture will become thick and glossy.

8 Continue cooking for another 20 minutes, stirring constantly. Check the set point with a candy thermometer (210°F).

9 Slowly ladle the jam into warm sterilized jars. Wipe the jar rims clean with a moist paper towel and screw the lids on tight. Store in cool dark place and consume within six months.

spiced pears in white wine

The abundance of fall pears is put to good use in this classic dessert recipe.

Ingredients

2 ½ lbs. ripe, firm Bartlett pears (about 6 small pears)

1 cup dry white wine

1½ cups raw cane sugar

2 cinnamon sticks

Pinch grated nutmeg

¼ teaspoon lemon zest

Juice 1 lemon

SERVES 6

Jeannette says

"choose a crisp, dry chardonnay wine for poaching pears."

day one

1. Wash pears in cold water. Peel the whole fruit leaving the stem intact.

2. Combine remaining ingredients in a preserve pan and bring to a boil on medium-low heat. Cook for about 15 minutes until the sugar dissolves, stirring gently and skimming off any foam that collects on the surface.

3. Place the pears, one by one, into the syrup mixture and poach over low heat until they are soft.

4. Use a slotted spoon to lift the pears and cinnamon sticks out of the syrup. Set aside.

5. Bring the syrup to a boil on medium heat. Reduce for 15 minutes until thickened.

6. Place the pears back into the syrup and reduce the heat to low. Simmer for 20 minutes, using a wooden spoon to gently turn the pears so they poach evenly.

7. Spoon individual pears into sterilized, widemouth canning jars and cover with syrup. Wipe the jar rims clean with a moist paper towel and screw the lids on tight. Store in a cool dark place and consume within six months.

spicy red pepper jelly

This piquant treat is best served with brie cheese and crackers, or used as a relish on roast chicken.

Ingredients

2 lbs. red bell peppers

3 tablespoons chopped Serrano peppers (seeds removed)

½ cup raw cane sugar

¾ cup cider vinegar

2 cups homemade pectin stock

YIELDS 6 X 6 OZ JARS

Jeannette says

"if you prefer more heat, substitute habanera chili peppers to taste."

day one

1. Wash the red bell peppers in cold water. Cut them in half. Remove the seeds and the white inner membrane. Puree in a food processor until smooth. Set aside.

2. In a preserve pan, combine the pectin stock, sugar, and apple cider vinegar. Bring to a simmer and cook for 25 minutes, skimming off any foam that collects on the surface.

3. Add the pureed red bell pepper and Serrano chili pepper. Bring to a boil over high heat for 10 minutes, stirring constantly.

4. Reduce to low heat and continue cooking for about 15 minutes until the mixture thickens. Skim as needed.

5. Check the set point (210°F), and continue cooking for another 2 minutes.

6. Carefully ladle the hot jelly into warm, sterilized jars. Wipe the jar rims clean with a moist paper towel and screw the lids on tight. Store in a cool dark place and consume within six months.

mango-ginger chutney

This classic preserve is divine served warm or chilled with sliced cold meats or Indian cuisine.

Ingredients

28 mangoes, medium-ripe

½ cup Thompson raisins

½ cup dried apricots

½ cup dried prunes

1 cup white wine vinegar

½ cup apple cider vinegar

2 teaspoons fresh ginger, minced

½ cup yellow onion, finely chopped

½ cup raw cane sugar

½ teaspoon black pepper

3 Serrano hot peppers, chopped

½ teaspoon kosher salt

YIELDS 6 X 9 OZ JARS

day one

1. Wash the mangoes. Remove the pit. Peel and cut into thin slices.

2. In a preserve pan, combine the mango slices, chopped onion, white wine & cider vinegars, salt, and sugar. Bring to a simmer for 20 minutes.

3. Add all the dried fruits and continue cooking on medium-low heat, stirring gently, until the liquid reduces and the mixture thickens.

4. Continue cooking and stirring gently for another 20 minutes. Add the black pepper, minced fresh ginger, and chopped Serrano pepper. Simmer until the chutney darkens and has a thick consistency.

5. Check the set point with a candy thermometer (210°F).

6. Slowly ladle the chutney into warm, sterilized jars. Wipe the jar rims clean with a moist paper towel and screw the lids on tight. Store in a cool dark place and consume within one year.

Jeannette says

"try flavoring this chutney with a little ground cardamom and coriander powder, which yields equally delicious results."

clementine & orange marmalade

This classic favorite preserve has a rich, sweet, and slightly tart flavor.

Ingredients

2 lbs. Clementine oranges

4 lbs. medium navel oranges

1 lb. Granny Smith apples

Juice 2 oranges

Juice 1 lemon

3 cups raw cane sugar

½ cup water

YIELDS 6 X 6 OZ JARS

Jeannette says

"you can substitute juicy Minneola tangelos (a hybrid citrus of tangerine and grapefruit) for the clementines in this recipe if desired."

day one

1. Rinse unpeeled apples in cold water. Remove the stems and cut into quarters. Place the apples in a large pot and add just enough water to cover them. Bring to a boil. Reduce to medium heat and simmer for 30 minutes.

2. Place a chinois sieve in a pan and pour the apple mixture into the sieve. Press lightly on the fruit with a wooden spoon to release all the juice into the pan. Set aside.

3. Squeeze the juice from (2) navel oranges and set aside. Bring a large pot of water to a rolling boil. Add the remaining whole navel oranges and boil 5-7 minutes until soft.

4. Use a wooden spoon to remove the oranges from the pot and plunge them in a cold water bath. Slice the oranges into very thin rounds.

5. Wash Clementines and cut into thin rounds.

6. In a preserve pan, combine the orange and Clementine slices with sugar and water. Bring to a simmer and cook on medium-low heat until the orange slices are translucent. Add the reserved apple juice, orange juice, lemon juice, and sugar.

7. Reduce heat to a simmer and continue cooking for 30 minutes, stirring gently with a wooden spoon and skimming off any foam that collects on the surface.

8. Pour the mixture into a bowl and cover with parchment paper. Refrigerate overnight.

day two

9. Pour the chilled mixture into a preserve pan and bring to a boil. Skim off any foam and continue cooking on high heat for 10-15 minutes, stirring frequently.

10. Reduce to low heat and continue cooking for another 15 minutes. The marmalade will become thick and glossy as it reduces. Check the set point with a candy thermometer (210°F) and test using the cold plate method (see A Note About the Set Point page 10).

11. Slowly ladle the marmalade into warm sterilized jars. Release air bubbles by running a clean knife around the rim of the marmalade.

12. Wipe the jar rims clean with a moist paper towel and screw the lids on tight. Store in a cool dark place and consume within six months.

pink grapefruit marmalade

Pink grapefruit stars with sweet Meyer lemons in this luscious topper for toast or poultry.

Ingredients

1 lb. unripe Granny Smith apples

3 ½ lbs. pink grapefruit

½ lb. Meyer lemons

3 cups raw cane sugar

Juice 1 grapefruit

½ cup water

YIELDS 6 X 6 OZ JARS

Jeannette says

"Use fresh, unripe apples which are naturally high in pectin for this recipe."

day one

1 Rinse the apples in cold water. Do not peel. Remove the stems and cut into quarters.

2 Put the apple segments in a large pot and cover them with water. Bring to a rolling boil. Reduce to medium heat and simmer until the apples are soft (about 30 minutes).

3 Set a fine-mesh chinois sieve in a large pan and pour the apple mixture into the sieve. Lightly press the fruit with the back of a wooden spoon to release all the juice into the collection pan. Set aside.

4 Squeeze the juice from 1 grapefruit and set aside. Reserve the grapefruit seeds and tie them in a small cheesecloth bag.

5 Wash the pink grapefruit and Meyer lemons in cold water. Cut into very thin round slices.

6 In a preserve pan, combine the grapefruit and lemon slices with 1 cup sugar and ½ cup water. Bring to a simmer and poach the fruit until translucent.

7 Add the reserved apple and grapefruit juice, 2 cups sugar, and the cheesecloth bag of seeds. Bring to a simmer and cook for 30 minutes, stirring gently with a wooden spoon and skimming off any foam that collects on the surface.

8 Pour the mixture into a bowl and cover with parchment paper. Refrigerate overnight.

day two

9 Pour the fruit preparation into a preserve pan and bring to a boil. Cook on high heat for 10 minutes, stirring gently and skimming off any foam.

10 Reduce to low heat and cook for another 15 minutes, stirring constantly to prevent scorching. The marmalade will become thick and clear with a rose hue. Remove the seed bag and check the set point with a candy thermometer (210°F).

11 Slowly ladle the marmalade into warm, sterilized jars. Wipe the jar rims clean with a moist paper towel and screw the lids on tight. Store in a cool dark place and consume within six months.

savory cranberry-apple-orange chutney

This chutney is sure to be a standout on your holiday table. Serve warm or chilled as a delicious accompaniment to roast turkey.

Ingredients

2 lbs. fresh cranberries

½ lb. Golden Delicious apples

Juice 2 oranges

grated zest ½ orange

½ yellow onion, diced

1 cup white wine vinegar

½ cup apple cider vinegar

½ cup raw cane sugar

¼ cup raisins

½ teaspoon cinnamon

¼ teaspoon ground cloves

2 Serrano peppers, diced small

¼ teaspoon kosher salt

YIELDS 6 X 6 OZ JARS

day one

1. Rinse the apples in cold water. Remove the stems, peels, and cores. Cut into thin slices and set aside.

2. Rinse the cranberries in cold water. Dry and set aside.

3. Wash the oranges in cold water. Grate the zest from ½ of 1 orange. Set aside. Squeeze the juice from the oranges and set aside. You should have about 1 cup juice.

4. Combine the cranberries, sliced apples, onion, wine and cider vinegars, and salt in a large preserve pan and bring to a boil. Cook for 15 minutes on medium heat until the fruits are soft.

5. Add the sugar, raisins, orange zest, and orange juice. Reduce heat to medium-low and simmer for 30 minutes, stirring gently with a wooden spoon.

6. Add the cinnamon, ground cloves, and diced Serrano peppers. Cook on low heat for 20 minutes, stirring gently as the mixture thickens.

7. Slowly ladle the chutney into warm sterilized jars. Wipe the jar rims clean with a moist paper towel and screw the lids on tight. Store in a cool dark place and consume within one year.

Jeannette says

"try adding walnuts or pistachios for extra texture and flavor."

JEANNETTE'S SEASONS OF JAM

Below is a list of the seasonal fruits I watch for as they arrive in farmers markets near me. Be sure to check your local farmers market for the freshest produce available, and always choose Certified Organic at the peak of ripeness to make the healthiest, most flavorful jam.

SPRING

LEMONS • RHUBARB • CHERRIES
STRAWBERRIES

SUMMER

NECTARINE • PEACH • FIGS • PLUMS
KIWI • MELONS • RASPBERRIES
APRICOT • PLUOTS • PRUNES

FALL

APPLES • PEARS • KUMQUATS
QUINCE • GOOSEBERRY
PUMPKIN • SQUASH • PEPPERS

WINTER

ORANGES • GRAPEFRUIT
CLEMENTINES • TANGERINES
CRANBERRIES

A Note About Measuring Ingredients

Measuring ingredients accurately is very important when making the recipes in this book. The following chart of equivalent measurements is provided for convenience.

Standard Liquid Measurements

1 tablespoon	3 teaspoons	½ fluid ounces
1/4 cup	4 tablespoons	2 fluid ounces
1/3 cup	5 1/3 tablespoons	2 ½ fluid ounces
½ cup	8 tablespoons	4 fluid ounces
2/3 cup	10 2/3 tablespoons	5 fluid ounces
3/4 cup	12 tablespoons	6 fluid ounces
1 cup	16 tablespoons	8 fluid ounces
1 pint	2 cups	16 fluid ounces
1 quart	2 pints	32 fluid ounces
1 gallon	4 quarts	128 fluid ounces

Standard Sugar Measurements

1 teaspoon	4 grams	0.15 ounces
1 tablespoon	12 grams	0.44 ounces
1/4 cup	50 grams	1.75 ounces
1/3 cup	66 grams	2.33 ounces
½ cup	99 grams	3.50 ounces
2/3 cup	132 grams	4.66 ounces
3/4 cup	149 grams	5.25 ounces
1 cup	198 grams	7.00 ounces

ACKNOWLEDGEMENTS

These pages are a testament to the many people who supported and encouraged me to follow my dream of creating this book of recipes. I am eternally grateful for their belief in my abilities, and their enthusiasm for this project.

My great respect and admiration goes to my publisher, Gaye Allen, for designing this beautiful book and patiently leading me through this process. She was a joy to work with and her considerable creative talents made my vision possible.

My deepest gratitude is saved for my editor/photographer, Karen Pavone, for her hard work, clarity, and attention to detail in developing the content on these pages. Her words and gorgeous photos brought my recipes to life!

My father taught me that "quality is quality"; simple and traditional is best. He instilled high standards in me and the belief that I could accomplish anything I set my mind to. This book honors his memory.

Warmest thanks to Gibson Thomas, Editor-in-chief at Edible Marin & Wine Country Magazine, who featured *Jeannette's Jams* in Edible's 2013 Winter Holiday Gift Guide. This generous publicity brought me and my products to a new audience at the Marin County Farmers Market in Corte Madera Town Center and Mill Valley.

A special thanks to my friends and family who are a constant source of inspiration; especially my daughter Julie, my daughter-in-law, Nadine La Bruno-Waller, and my niece, Sylvie Tran.

Finally, deepest thanks to my husband Robert for his love, encouragement, and support through the months as this book became a reality. Without Robert, there would be much less joy in my cooking!

HOW TO CONTACT *Jeannette* N'GUYEN HABIT

EMAIL: habit4@Jeannettejams.com

TELEPHONE: 415 234 6502